AURAL TEST SURVIVAL BOOK

Grade 1

Caroline Evans

EDITION PETERS

LONDON • FRANKFURT/M • LEIPZIG • NEW YORK

Peters Edition Limited
2-6 Baches Street
London
N1 6DN
England

Tel: +44 (0)20 7553 4000
Fax: +44 (0)20 7490 4921
e-mail: sales@editionpeters.com
Internet: www.editionpeters.com

First published 2006
Revised edition published 2012

ISBN 978-1-84367-040-7

A catalogue record for this book is available from the British Library

Cover design: www.adamhaystudio.com

Illustrations: Joy FitzSimmons

Printed in the UK by Halstan & Co Ltd, Amersham, Bucks.

CONTENTS

The *Aural Test Survival Book* offers a chapter-by-chapter look at responses to questions typically asked by examiners. The speed and accuracy of your responses will help you gain a better mark.

Key to Symbols

T Time

R Rhythm

K Key

About . . .
. . . the Aural Test Survival Book

Don't be scared of aural tests! The *Aural Test Survival Book* will help you improve your listening skills and prepare you for the aural test in your music exam. You can use this book with a teacher, parent or friend, or you can practise the exercises on your own.

This book will encourage you to listen to music more actively and give you confidence to tackle the aural tests in your exam.

Try to spend a little time on aural skills as part of your regular practice. You already have your examination pieces, studies and scales. Now here's your own book of aural skills!

Caroline Evans

A note to teachers

The material in the *Aural Test Survival Book* corresponds to the Associated Board's aural requirements for music examinations and is suitable for all instrumentalists. Many of the tests are common to other examination boards and so students preparing for any music exam will find the book useful.

You can try out the activities in your lessons, or you can set them for your students to complete at home. The format of the book encourages students to think in terms of three important elements of music: Time, Rhythm and Key.

When the examiner says:

"First, clap in time while I play. Join in as soon as you can and give a louder clap on the strong beats . . . Is it in two time or three time?"

What should you do?

Clap the beat of a short piece of music in 2- or 3-time.

When the music starts, join in as soon as possible, clapping the beat.

Clap louder on the strong beats.

You will then be asked to state the time: 2-time or 3-time. In other words, say whether there are 2 or 3 beats in a bar. You do not need to state the time signature.

What you need to know

BEAT is regular, like a clock ticking. RHYTHM is the varying note lengths and patterns within each beat. Make sure you clap the beat rather than the rhythm.

Always remember – rhythm varies but the beat is regular.

The passage of music will always start on the first beat of the bar.

How should you do it?

Before the music starts:
- Put your hands in position, ready to start clapping.

While listening:
- It may help to sway your body in time with the beat. Even better, tap your toe gently.
- Start counting in your head.
- Listen for the strong beats. These are usually on the first beat of the bar and will be slightly accented.
- Decide how many beats are in a bar.

When you start clapping:
- Clap the beat in time with the examiner. Don't clap the rhythm.
- Start clapping with the music as soon as you can.
- Clap loudly on the strong beats and lightly on the weaker beats.
- When you have finished clapping, state whether there are 2 or 3 beats in a bar.

At all times:

- **Stand tall**
- **Sound confident**
- **Speak out**

Training session

Music in 2-time

You may know the children's songs *Twinkle twinkle little star* and *Baa baa black sheep.* Sing them to yourself and march round the room in time. Stamp your foot on the strong beats. If you can't remember these songs, here are their rhythms and words:

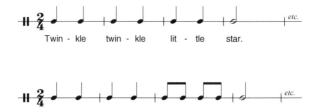

Now look at the rhythms again. Clap the beat, NOT the rhythm. The strong beats are marked with accents (>). Clap louder on the strong beats when you clap:

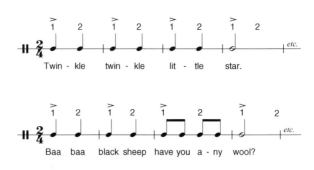

Now try counting three beats in a bar (1-2-3-1-2-3) to these songs; can you feel how the music doesn't fit?

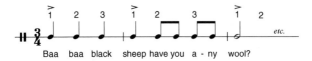

Finally, clap the beat in 2-time once more. Remember to clap louder on the strong beats. If you can remember the tunes, sing them at the same time.

Remember to clap on every beat, but louder on the strong beats.

Music in 3-time

If the music is in 3-time you won't be able to march to it (try marching to a tune in 3-time and see how the strong beat keeps falling on the opposite foot). Here are the rhythms and words of *Oranges and Lemons* and *Scarborough Fair*. These songs are both in 3-time:

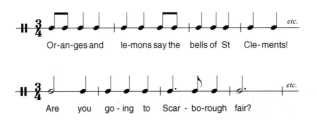

Now look at the rhythms again and clap the beat (not the rhythm). Clap louder on the strong beats – they are marked with accents (>):

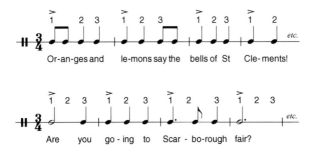

Now try counting two beats in a bar to these 3-time songs. Can you feel how the music doesn't fit?

Finally, clap the beat in 3-time once more. Remember to clap louder on the strong beats than on the weaker beats. If you can remember the tunes, sing them at the same time.

How to improve further

Every time you hear any music on the TV, radio, CD or mp3 player, clap the beat, or tap your toe. Try and work out how many beats there are in a bar.

The aim of the test

This test is designed to help you play your own pieces rhythmically and in time.

Quiz

Are the following in 2-time or 3-time? Answers on page 32.

1. *Pop Goes the Weasel*

2. *We wish you a merry Christmas*

3. *One potato, two potato, three potato, four . . .*

SURVIVAL TIPS

1. Be sure to clap the beat, NOT the rhythm.

2. When you clap, be precise; keep one hand still, palm upwards, and clap your other hand against it.

3. The strong beats will be slightly accented. Clap louder on the strong beats than on the weaker beats.

4. Start counting the beats in your head as soon as the music starts.

5. Work out whether the music is in two-time or three-time before the examiner asks you.

Clap in Time:

T Time: clap in time with the beat as soon as you can. Count the number of beats in a bar and state the time

R Rhythm: be aware of how the rhythm fits with the beat, but be sure to clap the beat, not the rhythm

SING ECHOES

When the examiner says:

"Next I'd like you to sing three phrases as echoes. Here is the key-chord . . . and your starting note . . ."

What should you do?

Sing, as "echoes", three short phrases played by the examiner. If you prefer, you may hum or whistle.

After each phrase is played, sing exactly what you have just heard played on the piano, immediately following on and in time with the beat. Each phrase will be within the range of a third (tonic to mediant).

Concentrate on the rhythm as well as the tune.

What you need to know

The three phrases will always be two bars long and in a major key.

The examiner will always start by playing the key-chord and the starting (tonic) note, and will then give a count-in of two bars (1-2-1-2 or 1-2-3-1-2-3).

The key-chord contains the first (tonic), third and fifth notes of the scale.

After the examiner has played each phrase, you should sing back as an echo "in time". This means you should keep in time with the beat started on the piano. Do not hesitate before you start.

How should you do it?

While listening:

- As soon as the examiner gives the count-in, gently tap your toe in time, right through to the end of the test.

- Listen carefully to the rhythm as well as the tune – the rhythm is just as important.

- Listen to the key-chord and starting (tonic) note, and keep them in mind throughout the test.

When you start singing:

- Keep tapping your toe gently in time while singing the echo.

- Sing "lah" to each note. If you prefer, you may hum or whistle, although it is very hard to whistle accurately.

- Don't pause after the examiner has finished playing – come straight in and keep to the same speed as the examiner.

- Keep the tonic note in your mind – it will also be your starting note.

- If you hear *staccato* (detached) notes, sing short notes.

- Don't cut short any notes that are long.

At all times:

- **Stand tall**
- **Sound confident**
- **Sing out**

Training session

Often your response to this test will be automatic. But here are a few steps to help sing back a tune accurately.

Play the first three notes of a G major scale (up and down) on your own instrument (if voice is your instrument, then sing). Play at a comfortable speed and tap your toe gently to keep in time.

If you play a bass-clef instrument, here is the same scale two octaves lower and in the bass clef:

When you have played this scale, sing it. In order for it to be comfortable for your voice, you may need to sing it an octave higher or lower than you played it.

Keep to the same speed you played before, and still tap your toe gently to keep in time. Sing "lah" or "doh" to each note, and make sure each note is separated.

As you sing, try to see the shape of the music in your head. It may help to draw the shape in the air with your hand. For example, if you play an ascending and descending scale, it will look like this:

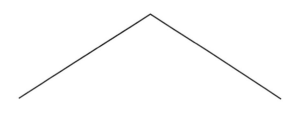

Look at the following music. The notes are the same as those in the scale you have just played and sung:

Start by clapping the rhythms of the notes printed, filling in the gaps by repeating (in other words, echoing) the printed rhythms. Don't leave a gap before your echo – keep to the same speed:

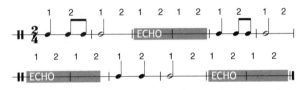

Now play the notes on your instrument, singing the echoes in the gaps. Remember to keep to the same speed. Play the notes of the key-chord first.

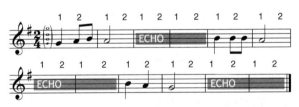

If you play a bass-clef instrument, here is the same music in the bass clef:

Now do the same with the following example. Start by clapping the rhythm, together with the echoes. Then play the music on your instrument and sing the echo. Remember to keep in time the whole way through. Count yourself in before you start.

Here is the same music two octaves lower and in the bass clef:

How to improve further

Play the first two bars of a piece you are learning and sing them back. Then do the same for another two bars in the same piece.

Listen to some music you don't know and practise singing back short phrases. You could use the radio or TV and press the mute button while you sing echoes.

The aim of the test

This test is designed to develop your melodic memory.

Quiz

Draw the shape (either on paper or in the air with your hand) of the opening bars of the following songs. Answers on page 32.

1. *Nellie the elephant*

2. *Frère Jacques*

3. *Three blind mice*

SURVIVAL TIPS

1. Don't worry about the sound of your voice; concentrate on singing in tune and in time.

2. Even if you feel nervous, try to *appear* confident. Sing out – a loud mistake is better than a quiet one.

3. Use bright vowels – "lah" is usually best.

4. If you hear *staccato* notes, sing short notes.

5. Try to hear the notes in your head while you listen.

6. It may help to follow the shape of the phrase with your hand as you listen and sing.

7. Sing something, even if you're unsure.

Follow the TRaK:

T Time: tap your toe in time with the beat while listening and singing

R Rhythm: listen carefully to the rhythm as well as the tune and don't cut long notes short

K Key: listen carefully to the key-chord and tonic note – the tonic note will also be your starting note. Sing in tune.

When the examiner says:

"Now I'll play a phrase twice, but with a change to one of the notes the second time. Tell me whether the change was near the beginning or near the end. Here is the key-chord . . . and the tonic . . . And now with the change . . . Was the change near the beginning or near the end?"

What should you do?

Spot the difference in pitch (higher or lower notes) of a two-bar phrase played twice.

Decide where you heard the changed note.

What you need to know

The examiner will start by playing the key-chord and the first (tonic) note of the scale, then give a count-in of two bars (1-2-1-2, 1-2-3-1-2-3 or 1-2-3-4-1-2-3-4) before playing the first version.

The two-bar phrase, which will be in a major key, will be played twice, with a change in the second playing.

One of the notes will be either lower or higher when the examiner plays the phrase the second time. Only one note is changed; you just need to say where the change took place.

Both versions will be played a second time if necessary, although this will affect your mark.

How should you do it?

While listening:

- Decide whether the change was near the beginning or near the end of the music.

When you answer:

- Tell the examiner whether the change was made near the beginning or near the end of the music.

- Answer straight away.

At all times:

- **Stand tall**
- **Sound confident**
- **Speak out**

Training session

Play this short phrase on your instrument. Before you start, choose a comfortable speed. Clap the rhythm before you play.

J. S. Bach

If you play a bass-clef instrument, here is a version two octaves lower and in the bass clef.

Test 1C

Keeping to the same speed, play this slightly different version.

Here is a bass-clef version:

Did you notice that in the second bar the note pitch on the second beat was different from the one in the first version? In this case, when the examiner asks whether the change was near the beginning or near the end, you should say "near the end".

Remember, you don't need to say whether the difference in pitch is higher or lower. You just have to state where the difference is.

Now play these two phrases. Once again, choose a comfortable speed. Clap the rhythm first.

Here are the same phrases in the bass clef:

This time you should hear a change near the beginning.

Here is the opening of a song from Northumberland which may be familiar to you. Clap the rhythm first. Sing or play it on your own instrument.

Here is a bass clef version:

Now sing or play this second version.

Here is the same phrase in the bass clef:

The rhythms are exactly the same in both phrases, but one note pitch is different. Can you spot the difference? Where did it change?

Reading and playing the music yourself will help you describe where the pitch change took place.

Test 1C

If you prefer, you can raise your hand while the music is playing, to show where the difference is.

Now play these two phrases and describe where the change takes place. Practise saying it out loud. Before you play the phrases, clap the rhythms.

Here are the same phrases in the bass clef:

How to improve further

Play short phrases from pieces you know very well. Make up your own changes of pitch, changing just one note. Practise saying out loud whether the change is near the beginning or near the end of the phrase.

The aim of the test

The purpose of this test is to develop your awareness of pitch.

1. You may find that closing your eyes helps you to concentrate.

2. Simply state *where* you hear the change - near the beginning or near the end.

3. If you can't hear the change the first time, don't be afraid to ask the examiner to play the phrases again, although this will affect your mark.

4. Don't worry if the examiner doesn't tell you that you are right – this doesn't mean that you have got it wrong.

DESCRIBE THE MUSIC

When the examiner says:

"Listen to this piece, then I'll ask you about loud or quiet playing and about smooth or detached notes."

What should you do?

The examiner will play a short piece of music and then ask you about two features. The first feature will be:

Loud or quiet
   (sometimes described as dynamics)

Gradually getting louder or quieter

The second feature will be:

Detached or smooth
   (sometimes described as articulation)

What you need to know

The first feature to listen for will be dynamics: whether the music is loud or quiet; or if there are sudden or gradual changes. The second feature will be articulation: whether the music is deatched or smooth.

You should try to know the meaning of the following Italian words. But if you can't remember the Italian word, use the English.

Loud or quiet

   loud
   Italian: *forte*
   symbol: f

quiet
Italian: *piano*
symbol: p

Gradually getting louder or quieter

gradually getting louder
Italian: *crescendo*
symbol: ───── (an "opening hairpin")

gradually getting quieter
Italian: *diminuendo*
symbol: ═════ (a "closing hairpin")

Detached or smooth

detached
Italian: *staccato*
symbol: ♪ ♩

smooth
Italian: *legato*
symbol: ⌒ (a slur)

How should you do it?

Before the music starts:

- You only need to listen for two features; the examiner will tell you which BEFORE the music starts.

While listening:

- Concentrate only on the particular musical features specified.

When you answer:

- Answer straight away.

- State even what seems obvious.

- Try to use Italian words like *forte, piano, crescendo, diminuendo, staccato* and *legato* in your answers, but using English words is acceptable.

Training session

Play the following piece of music on your instrument, or sing it.

Or, in the bass clef:

Now play it *forte* and *piano*:

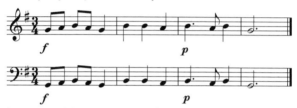

Answer this question about what you have just played:

"The piece began loudly. How did it finish?"

Now play it with a *crescendo* and *diminuendo*:

Answer this question:

"The piece began quietly. Did it gradually get louder anywhere?"

Finally play it with *staccato* and *legato* notes:

Answer this question:

"The piece started with detached notes. Were the notes in the second half of the piece detached or smooth?"

Listen to some music on the radio or on a CD. Think about the different ways you have just played and decide whether the music you are listening to is:

> loud (*forte*) or quiet (*piano*)

> getting gradually louder (*crescendo*) or gradually quieter (*diminuendo*)

> detached (*staccato*) or smooth (*legato*)

Practise saying the answers out loud even if you are on your own. This is important because saying the answer is very different from thinking about the answer.

Here are some examples of questions you might be asked, and the sort of words you could use to answer them:

Loud or quiet

Question: "Where was the quietest part of the music?"
Answer: "It was quietest in the middle."

Question: "The piece was loud at the beginning. Did it stay loud all the way through?"
Answer: "No. It was quiet, or *piano* at the end."

Gradually getting louder or quieter

Question: "The piece began quietly. Did it gradually get louder anywhere?"
Answer: "Yes. In the middle there was a *crescendo*."

Question: "Towards the end, did the piece get *suddenly* or *gradually* quieter?"
Answer: "It got gradually quieter. There was a *diminuendo*."

Detached or smooth

Question: "Were the notes smooth or detached?"
Answer: "They were detached, or *staccato*."

Question: "When the music was quiet, were the notes smooth or detached?"
Answer: "They were smooth, or *legato*."

At all times:

- **Stand tall**
- **Sound confident**
- **Speak out**

How to improve further

At the beginning of the day, choose one musical feature (loud or quiet; gradually getting louder or softer; detached or smooth). Whenever you hear some music during that day, use a single sentence to describe that feature. On the next day, choose a different feature and do the same thing.

The aim of the test

This test is designed to encourage you to *listen* to music rather than just hearing it.

1. Say SOMETHING – you may get something right. But if you say nothing you will certainly get nothing right.

2. If you can't remember the Italian word, say it in English.

3. The questions you will be asked usually require only one-word or very short answers.

4. If you are a woodwind player, you may prefer to use the word "tongued" instead of detached (*staccato*).

5. The examiner will only use straightforward words like "gradually louder" and "gradually quieter" (or "softer").

FIND OUT THE MEANING

This list contains the words you should know for Grade 1, and their meanings. In your answers, try to use the proper words (in blue) wherever possible.

◁

This sign is referred to as an "opening hairpin" and means *crescendo*, or gradually getting louder

▷

This sign is referred to as a "closing hairpin" and means *diminuendo*, or gradually getting quieter

>

Accent

Allegro

Quick, lively

Andante

At a walking speed

Articulation

How the notes are played or sung (smoothly or detached)

Beat

A unit of time. In 4/4 time there are four crotchet beats in a bar. Sometimes the word "pulse" is used for "beat"

Crescendo, cresc.

Gradually getting louder

Diminuendo, dim.

Gradually getting quieter

Dynamics

How loudly or quietly the notes are played or sung

Forte, _f_
>   Loud

Home note
>   First note of the scale, or **tonic**

Key
>   This can be major or minor. It also applies to the sharps (♯) or flats (♭) in the key signature

Key-chord
>   The first, third and fifth notes of the scale

Key note, tonic
>   First note of the scale, or **home note**

Legato
>   Smooth

Moderato
>   At a moderate speed

Piano, _p_
>   Quiet, soft

Pitch
>   How high or low a note is

Rhythm
>   Notes of varying length grouped into patterns

Staccato
>   Detached

Tonic, key note
>   First note of the scale, or **home note**

Note
>   The words used to introduce the tests may differ slightly to those used in this book.

Page 10

   1. 2-time
   2. 3-time
   3. 2-time

Page 16

1.

2.
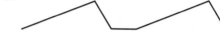

3.